MW01277254

POCKET MONOLOGUES:
WORKING-CLASS CHARACTERS
for WOMEN

Susan Pomerance

Dramaline Publications

Dramaline Publications
36-851 Palm View Road, Rancho Mirage, CA 92270

**Library of Congress
Cataloging-in-Publication Data**

Pomerance, Susan.
    Pocket Monologues:Working-Class Characters for Women/Susan Pomerance—Rancho Mirage, CA: Dramaline Publications, 1999
        ISBN 0-940669-40-4 (alk. paper)
        I. Title.   98-23221

Cover art by John Sabel

CONTENTS

Foreword

The speeches in this book were deliberately written in extended lengths. This was done in the interest of delving into each character to a degree that would reveal more of her true nature and also allow for the unfolding of a mini-story. Realizing that time constraints are often placed on auditions and presentations, each monologue is presented in an "uncut" and "cut" version by the placement of bold brackets ([ ]) around the portion of the speech to be omitted.

If you wish to cut these speeches even further, please do so judiciously and in a manner that will not disrupt continuity.

CLARA
(Waitress)

Clara works at the White Front Cafe, a clean-as-a-pin eatery in a small Midwestern city. She has been employed there for years and has seen a lot of life. Nothing much rattles or gets past Clara. Here she speaks of her encounter with a group passing through town on its way to Chicago.

CLARA

[How 'bout a little slice o' peach pie, Willard? Fresh outta the oven no more'n an hour ago. Still warm. *(she pauses for Willard's reply)*

Okay, suit yerself. *(she wipes the counter top)*]

I tell ya what we had in here yesterday? We had a real bunch, I'll tell ya, a sure enough real bunch. They come a-rollin' in 'bout a half past four on their way inta Chicaga. Was drivin' from Cincinnata in one o' them big German cars. You know, the kind with the front end that looks like a Bar-B-Q grill. *(she pauses for his reaction)*

Yeah, a Mer-ca-dees. One o' them. [They pass ever'thing but a gas station, I understand. According t' Lloyd Carnes, that is.] Anyway, here they come, all dressed up an' a-paradin' along like store dummies with their noses up in the air like they was runnin' from a skunk or somethin'. [They set down big as ya please right over there in the corner booth, an' when I brung 'em water they looked at me like I was dirty laundry.]

You shoulda seen how they was dressed. You know your *Star Trek* series? Well, their outfits were kind a like that. They was all ready for outer space, lemme tell ya. Where the devil they get some o' these outfits these days beats me. Mebbe from the Ringling Brothers. [The woman had this orange hair on her that stuck out like spikes all over 'er head. She looked like a neon porcupine. An' 'er dress was so short she'd been better off wearin' a string around 'er waist.

2

Didn't leave much t' the imagination. And the fellas had these here baggy suits on 'em that must a been left over from Halloween.]

Well, they come in an' look over the menu, an' can't make up their minds what they want, an' keep askin' me all these silly questions: "Is yer food salt-free?" "Ya got Perrier?" "Is yer milk raw?" "Ya got naturally grown vegetables?" They was worried t' death 'bout pesticides an' red meat an' the local water an' saturated fats an' sugar an' caffeine an' nitrites an'— you name it, brother. [Why, hell, they couldn't eat anything. No wonder they looked like they did. Like the color o' wet paper. Not a pretty sight.]

When I told 'em all we had was jus' regular food like ham on rye an' cheeseburgs an' pie an' the like, they all shrunk back in the booth like someone had pulled a gun on 'em. And when I said "hot fudge," I thought they was gonna have a shit-hemorrhage.

[They kept on 'bout natural foods an' all that till I'd had enough. People like that ain't got a

3

clue or don't give a damn for people who get up before breakfast and put in ten hours fer peanut wages. I'd been here since six an' I wasn't about t' stand around discussin' "health food" with a bunch a weirdos. Besides, these here people in big cars and clown outfits don't tip worth a crap. They're as cheap as they are silly.]

So, then, I say, "Look, folks, what we got here is regular everday food that's full o' grease and drippin' with fat an' loaded with flavor that'll make ya burp later and remind ya ya had good eatin'. If ya want rabbit food, I suggest ya mosey on down t' the feed store an' pick up a couple a bales o' straw. [Now ya wanna place yer order or not? If not, I got me people here with natural appetites who're watin' for an honest meal."] Well, you'd think I'd just pulled the plug on their bath water, or somethin'. They got real indignant an' stalked out like a parade o' penguins and got in their Mer-ca-dees an' drove off on down the interstate. Weird.

We get these nuts in here ever' now an' then. I guess this is what happens to ya when ya listen t' too much rock 'n' roll. More coffee?

ALICE
(Auto Worker)

Alice is employed as an inspector at an auto manufacturing plant. She is a conscientious person who is intolerant of shoddy workmanship, a characteristic that brings her into conflict with her co-workers (especially men) who resent Alice's criticism not because it's unwarranted, but because it comes from a woman who is performing a "man's job."

ALICE

I've been here at the plant for almost fifteen years. I started on the line applying molding and trim and doing finishing applications. [I started working here after my husband passed away unexpectedly. I had three young children and very little money and I had to get out and hustle in order to keep things going. At first, I felt out of place here because the whole manufacturing environment was foreign to me. After being

6

"just a housewife" for years I wasn't prepared for anything outside domestic work. But I knew I'd never be able to make ends meet doing housework. That kind of work is back-breaking and pays nothing and it leads nowhere.]

I've worked myself up to inspector. I have final say over the interiors, how things match up and fit. Like a dashboard, for instance. It has to be perfectly aligned and all spacings should be symmetrical and tight. Usually, there's no problem.

American workmanship has gotten much better in the past few years. But occasionally, cars come down the line that don't pass muster. Sloppy installations. So, when they do, I write 'em up and the work has to be done over. That's when sometimes it hits the fan. [Some people get ticked-off and bitch and raise all kinds of hell and accuse me of being overly picky and unreasonable. Hey, I'll admit, I *am* unreasonable when it comes to sloppy workmanship. There's no excuse for it—ever.]

In the beginning, it was really hell down here. Because there were these guys who came down on me like you wouldn't believe. [I nearly asked for my old job back in finishing. But then I came to realize that the people who were bitching were the same ones who bitched time after time, and that they were all men. I wrote up women, too, but I seldom heard complaints from them.]

At one point, some of these jokers became so hostile and threatening and abusive that I brought it before the plant foreman. He called a meeting where the bitchers had a chance to air their grievances. But they didn't have any legitimate beefs because all of the jobs I wrote up were justified and the foreman came down on my side and chastised the living hell out of these characters for harassing me. What was at the bottom of it was their inability to take on-the-job criticism from a woman. All of this came out, pouring out inadvertently at the meeting. All of the ingrained hostilities and petty hatreds instilled from childhood about the "proper" roles for men and women came running from their mouths in this flood of hysterical prejudice. [It was amazing. You know, I actually felt embarrassed for them.]

I still get the gripes. And, oh sure, sometimes for the same old stupid reasons. [But not as often now. Even though some of the guys still resent having their work judged by a woman.]

But, little by little, they've come to respect me even though a lot of them still have this resentment and these old-fashioned ideas. Because they know I'm a pro, and that I'm experienced. And they know I'm fair.

Women . . . we have indeed come a long way.

STELLA
(Truck Driver—Short-Haul)

Stella Valenziano was born and raised and still resides in the Bronx, where she has a good-paying job as a local-haul truck driver, an occupation that suits her aggressive, outgoing nature.

STELLA

They said I couldn't handle this job. Shows what they know. [Shows they're full of it. People get ideas, ya know. Get fixed in their thinking and are hard to bust loose from old attitudes. Heads like stale bread, you know. *(pointing to her head)* Oatmeal up here. Runny eggs.]

Like my husband, Ralph. The day I went to work he wouldn't speak to me. [He just got up in the morning and ate his usual ten pounds of fat and went off to work pouting. Just like a little kid. Only little kids have a sense of humor.]

Ralph couldn't accept the fact I was going to drive a truck for a living. Said it wasn't ladylike.

When I told him that there were lots of women pushing rigs who were top performers he said it was because they wore tattoos and were all named Bert. [He said I was too small and too fragile. He just couldn't accept the fact that you can be feminine and do a man's job.]

What's the big deal about driving a truck, anyway? You get in and start it up and throw it in gear and go. Like what does a truck know? Like a truck can tell it's being shifted by a woman? Nonsense.

[Sometimes I do get strange looks from men, though. They see me coming down the street in this tank and they can't believe it. It threatens them to see a woman hauling ass. They get this look on their faces like they've just seen their old lady with another guy, or something. Alluva sudden their male world is pulled out from under them. Not all men, just some, the ones still living on the edges of the last century.]

I like this job a lot. It's really neat. I get to get out there and hustle and make things happen because with delivery you're responsible for getting things to people that are important to them. The stuff you deliver says something. It says, "Here I am, what you've been waiting for." Delivery is what makes this country happen. [I saw this sign on the side of a truck once that said it all. It said, "If you have it, a truck brought it." Hey, is this profound, or what? Think about it.]

I'm proud of my job and proud of the way I do it. I can put this truck anywhere. Get it as close to a wall as a coat of paint. Over in Queens the other day, I had to back a load of Levis down this narrow alleyway to a loading dock. No room to screw up, no tolerance for error. Tight as a virgin. But I backed it right in there the first time. The guys on the dock couldn't believe it. [Said that the week before it took this dude half an hour to back his truck in there. And his rig was smaller, too. They were amazed. Said they didn't know how I did it without a good coat of Vaseline.]

After I'd slipped it in there on the first try they all stood there and applauded me. It was kind of like I'd just done this big acting scene out of Shakespeare, or something, you know. The only difference is, now that I think back on it, maybe what I did was even better than Shakespeare. Hey, with Shakespeare you don't get Levis.

ESTHER
(Retail Checker)

Esther is a check-out person at a large discount store, an establishment that sells "everything."

ESTHER

They come in. They buy. They buy everything. Junk, mostly. We get junk in by the carload and put it on display and it goes like snow in August.

Yesterday we got in a hundred dozen of these little coffee mugs that were made in Taiwan that were in these sickening pastel colors that would make you barf; with ugly little flower designs all over 'em that would rub off if you put any pressure on 'em. Well, the assistant put out a couple hundred yesterday morning and by noon they were all gone. [People snapped 'em up like they were the greatest thing since Kleenex. It's hard to figure. It seems like the junkier stuff is the faster it walks out the door.] I guess this is because we're a discount store and people just assume that the stuff we carry is a real deal.

[And of course, face it, we don't get your Neiman-Marcus-type shopper here. Our customers are bargain conscious; they're shopping for price. And they try to get away with murder. They change price tags and shoplift and try to return stuff after they've had it for months. The other day, this little old lady came in complaining that the pantyhose we sold her were cheap and didn't hold up. When I told her to bring 'em back, she said, "I did." Then she goes and pulls up her dress and shows 'em to me. Just like that, right there in the checkout line with a least twenty people behind her. I told her, "Lady, you have to take 'em *off* to return 'em, for Pete's sake."]

Working as a checker, I see all kinds. [They all come through here: the shorts, the regulars, and the extra-longs. With brains to match. It's a real study in human nature.] Like some of the men when they come through the check-out line with condoms—they're so embarrassed it isn't funny. They try to hide them under other merchandise so the other customers won't know they're buying them. They go bananas when I call out the item when I ring it up: "Deodorant $1.79, shampoo $2.99, Trojans $8.95." Their faces turn the color of rotten eggplant.

Then you get the dips who flaunt it. "Are these any good?" "Ever try this brand?" This one dork actually asked if we carried 'em in extra-large. Men. [Of course, some of the women are just as off-the-wall. The thing they do that ticks me off the most is when they put everything back in their purse before moving on. They take their change, they fold their bills, they put them in their wallets, close the wallets, put the wallets in their purses, snap the purses. All this while eighteen impatient bargain hunters are lined up behind them.]

Being a checker is no picnic, let me tell you. You're on your feet eight hours a day five days a week, and you get all kinds of strangies and weirdos and lots of complaints and grief. And through it all you're expected to remain calm and polite and stand there with this big happy smile on your face at all times. Ridiculous!

But the pay's not bad and we're union and we receive excellent benefits. Like free dental care, complete medical, and so on. *(she reflects)* Hum . . . I wonder if they cover cosmetic surgery. If so, maybe I'll get me a smile implant.

SAMANTHA
(Window Washer)

Samantha, a well-educated woman from a monied family, washes windows in high-rise buildings. It's a job eschewed by many due to apparent risks and a natural tendency for acrophobia and attendant vertigo. But Samantha relishes her job far above the maddening crowd.

SAMANTHA

I've had a romance with tall buildings ever since I was a kid. Yes, even as a child I remember looking up at skyscrapers and marveling at their grandeur, their stature and power. [I saw them as these gigantic glass and steel fingers pointing heavenward.]

I used to spend hours marveling at buildings. I was magnetized by them, drawn upward into them as though I were part of them. I know this all sounds pretentiously poetic and probably inane, but I actually do relate to these structures the way lots of people do to nature or religion. [I find in them this overwhelming, silent majesty, this tranquillity, this power and reassuring strength.]

Even though they're man-made, great buildings seem to take on a life of their own, a personality. I know I'm in the minority on this, but I've never thought of great buildings as just unfeeling, imposing structures put here to house workaday activities. To me they're positive monuments to what man can accomplish. They're like . . . like tributes to the better side of us, the constructive side, the creative.

[Just take a good look at a great building sometime. Instead of just walking past, take time to back off and look upward. Let the building take you with it on its climb skyward. Ride it upwards as it narrows, rising in perspective. Imagine that it doesn't stop, that it continues to rise beyond its uppermost floor in this unseen line that ultimately penetrates the universe and its riddles. Let your imagination go. Try it.]

For a while, after leaving college with a degree in Renaissance Literature, I kind of floundered around aimlessly, living off family money, pretending to be this heavy intellectual. In truth, I was a big pain in the ass who didn't have a clue about anything.

Then, one day, I went on a job interview for a major company that had its executive offices on the top floor of one of our tallest buildings. From the office windows you could see the city stretching out below like this vast, intricate, urban carpet. Outside the window, suspended from a scaffold, were people washing it. Right away I got this chill, this kind of rush from the idea of maintaining a giant like this. Wow! What a job, I thought. And one that's certainly not your run-of-the-mill occupation. Well, I didn't hang around for the interview.

I've been a window washer for about three and a half years, and I still get a rush every time I go up there. [My family and friends think I'm out of it, think I'm eccentric, you know. But, what the hell—they always did, anyway. It's difficult for them, for most people, to understand my love for great buildings and the thrill I get from my intimacy with them.]

When I'm washing windows it's like I'm involved with something special. And another thing: When I'm up there on that scaffold, hanging out there forty stories high, I feel free, liberated. It's kind of like I'm out there swinging on a dream.

JAN
(Construction Worker)

Early each workday, Jan slips into her jeans, work shirt, and safety boots and goes to a construction site somewhere in the city. She works alongside men at a job they have dominated for decades, finding satisfaction and fulfillment in her labors.

JAN

(as she speaks she slips into heavy safety boots) I'm on my way over to the north side. I'm working on some new condos that are going up over there. [They're going to sell for four hundred thousand dollars, minimum. They're for people with money. I wouldn't know, myself. Even though I knock down a pretty good salary I couldn't afford one. And, besides, four hundred thousand for one of those places? Forget it. They're not worth it. It must be the location.

*(stands and laces her boots by alternately plac-
ing them on a chair)*]

I'm out of here by six-thirty every morning. I
get up at five. [I don't like to rush, never did. I
like to have a solid breakfast, take a look at the
paper, watch a little TV. When I was working in
the office, I used to take even more time because
of my hair.]

One of the good things about this job is you
don't have to worry about your hair, because nobody sees it under a hard hat. *(displays her
hands)* And nails? Forget it. Hey, what are nails?
(resumes lacing her boots)

Appearances aren't all that important when
you're throwing a load of two-by-fours off the
back of a flat-bed. [And even though you wear
gloves, your hands take a pretty good beating.
But, what the hell?] Besides, it's kind of nice not
having to worry about hair and hands and what
clothes you're going to wear every day. It's a
relief not standing in front of your closet for
twenty minutes every morning trying to figure
out how to arrange a nothing wardrobe so it

won't look like you've worn the same combination two days in a row. *(stuffs her work shirt into her jeans)*

[I own five pairs of Levis, a pair of safety shoes, five work shirts, a jacket, and a pair of leather gloves. The company furnishes the hard hat.]

I'm the only woman they've got out on construction. I used to be in the office, but I got damned sick and tired of inhaling stale air and sitting in front of a computer all day. My butt was getting wider than my chair. Office work is very debilitating. *(goes to a rack holding her jacket)*

When I asked for a transfer to construction, I got some strange looks from the other women in the office. [Apparently they received the wrong signal. Here was a lady who all of a sudden wanted to start slipping a pinch of Skoal between her cheek and gum, right? They were very suspicious and kind of standoffish after that.] But I didn't take offense. Why should I? I could understand. It isn't every day a woman decides to unload sacks of cement for a living. And Brian, my guy, he really got uptight. He's an A-number-one yuppie. The thought of me working next to guys who didn't wear beepers really blew his mind. *(removes a heavy denim jacket from the rack and pulls it on)*

At first it was pretty rough. I used muscles that apparently belonged to somebody else. [I hurt from head to toe, every inch of me. And I got these blisters on my hands that raised up like big pink biscuits. I'd stagger back here at night and sit in a tub of hot water and go to bed at nine. To be perfectly honest, I didn't think I'd make it. For the first few weeks, I was one great big aching zombie who nearly became a lonely aching zombie because Brian said he was going to call it quits if I didn't stop falling asleep over dinner.] But, little by little, I toughened up and the blisters turned to calluses and the pain turned to muscle. And now, now I can keep up with the best of them. Yesterday I helped unload a semi full of drywall.

And Brian, he's accepted the change and we're getting along great. Except when I beat him at arm wrestling, that is. *(places a hard hat on her head and exits)*

TINA
(Taxi Driver)

*Tina pushes her hack around Los Angeles. Being
from a small town, she sometimes finds it difficult to relate to LA. types. But she is savvy and is
not intimidated by the bizarre elements of the
Los Angeles lifestyle.*

TINA

My hometown is Flagstaff. A nice, comfortable
town, but the money there is nothing. Driving a
cab out there is this low-stress, low-paying experience. Last year I made just over twelve thousand dollars. People don't think taxis in Flag.
They think horses and bowling and going down
to Wendy's for a burger and fries. [It's a
growing community, but it's still basically a
small college town. Also, it gets pretty crappy up
there during the winter. Seven-thousand feet
spells death to your Italian shoes.] But the

people are nice and laid-back and not freaky. Like here.

Coming to LA. after Flagstaff is future shock. Like two different worlds. You almost need a passport to make the move, I swear. When I first got here I applied for a job with a cab company in the Valley. They hired me right away because I have experience. I guess that's the reason. Either that or it's because I'm the only driver they have who doesn't look like he just broke out of the San Diego Zoo. We've got some real weirdos.

Some of the fares I get here you wouldn't believe. LA. is a great big bowl of mixed nuts. Last week I picked up this strange guy in Hollywood who's with a woman at least thirty years younger who had eyes that looked like they weren't connected to her brain. She kept calling the guy "Little Puppy." He wasn't so little, but he was sure a dog, all right. I took them to a seedy motel in Studio City. Who knows? Strange. In this business you don't make judgments.

And then, of course, there's the way they drive out here. [It's kind of like automobile bumper pool. In Flagstaff a caution light means slow up and stop. Out here it means "floor it baby and hope for the best." It's like intersection derby, you know. And then there's the freeways where it's either dead-stop or pedal-to-the-metal or some nut blowing your brains out because he doesn't like your hairdo.] Driving a cab in Los Angeles is a high-risk business that requires razor-sharp reflexes, stamina, and a thirst for adventure.

But I can't complain about the money. There's no comparison to Flagstaff. But driving these suicide missions five days a week is starting to take its toll. I woke up the other night in a cold sweat after having this nightmare about running down Tom Cruise.

I think maybe it's time to head on back to Arizona.

DORIS
(Policewoman)

Doris, a very feminine officer, speaks of her profession.

DORIS

My friends say, "Why in the world would you want to be a cop?" They have a hard time coming to grips with my profession. And when I tell strangers what I do for a living, they look at me like I'm from outer space. I guess this is because I don't fit their image of what a policewoman should look like: six feet two with wrists like bedposts. [I think most people have this pre-set idea that a lady officer has to be built like a professional wrestler. To them, "cop" means "brute."]

Size is the very least of it. Common sense is the main factor. Like using your smarts in crisis situations to keep them low-key and under control, to resolve them with a minimum of conflict and, at the same time, keep from getting messed up or blown away. Police work is a lot more than a matter of macho heroism, let me tell you—much more. [You never, under any circumstances, want to project a militant attitude. This is senseless and wasteful and proves zip. And you don't jump into life-threatening situations without giving a lot of thought to the consequences. The last thing you want is to become an instant statistic.]

We're highly trained to deal with problems on every level; problems from minor traffic violations to ones involving riots, murder—you name it. And each incident presents a particular set of circumstances that has to be dealt with degrees of firmness, restraint, force, and psychology. [The job demands a cool head at all times. The good cops are the ones who know how to keep a low profile while getting the job done.]

It's not an easy job and there are certainly risks—plenty. But you confront a variety of situations and this is what makes the job so interesting. Police work is very challenging and rewarding.

But, of course, there are the jobs that get to you. Like the death verification calls, for instance. This usually means going to a convalescent home and identifying the body of an elderly person and making sure there are no signs of foul play. This is one job that makes me cringe. Not dealing with death necessarily, but going into that situation, that environment, those homes. [They're so depressing and they all seem to have this specific odor that's a mixture of Pine-Sol and medicine. And here you have these pitiful, fragile old people living out what's left of their lives.] It can be very unsettling. But the thing that gets to me more than anything is the incidents involving children. They're the worst, the most emotionally loaded. Even after all these years, I still haven't gotten used to them.

But then there are the good aspects, the rewarding parts of the job: Reviving people, for instance, seeing them come back, knowing you've played a part in it and seeing the look of relief on the faces of loved ones; reassuring people in distress, bringing them comfort; helping people in trouble and getting involved and sometimes making a difference. [These are just a few of the benefits that offset the hard side and make it all worthwhile.]

Sometimes my friends get on my case and get off on calling me "Lady Copper," "The Fuzz," "Lawman," you name it. I get plenty of good-natured heat. But it doesn't bother me, not in the least. I just shine it on.

I'm proud of my profession.

MARY
(Cleaning Lady)

Mary has discovered that when it comes to people, "The rule is—there's no rule."

MARY

I guess you might say I owe my profession to other people's prosperity. And frequently their laziness.

When people are wealthy they don't want anything to do with housework. When you're loaded, getting down on your knees to scrub around your toilet is out of the question. [And, hey, I can understand this. I mean, why would you clean up your own john if you could afford to hire someone to do it for you?]

[Then, like I said, you've got the people who are just plain lazy, the ones who won't lift a hand to do anything they don't have to. Like this one client we have who sits in her den eating junk food and watching soaps and talk-shows all

34

day long. She never leaves her TV, not for a second. She has to be asked to raise her feet so we can vacuum under them. She's a TV junkie. Although, I'm not complaining. Oh, no. The richies and lazies of this world are great for business.]

The way some people live you wouldn't believe. Like pigs, in a constant state of disorder, who don't clean or touch a thing from one week to another. And some of the places look like everything's been thrown up in the air and let fall where-the-hell-ever. It's hard to believe that people can do that much damage in just seven days. Sometimes I think they must hire a wrecking crew to come in and do professional damage.

And you talk about filth! Good Lord! I swear, I don't know how some people live like they do—with clutter and dust and dirt and odors that would melt the horn off of a rhino. But, after all, it's nothing to me. I mean, this is what they're paying us for, right? [Besides, I shouldn't be so damned judgmental. But you'd think if people had any pride at all they'd want to live like human beings instead of porkers.]

And money, money has nothing to do with it, nothing at all. In fact, some of our richest customers are the filthiest. You can't judge the way people live, or the way they relate to you, from the size of their bank account. Some of the smallest customers treat you the worst. While, on the other hand, some of the wealthiest are the nicest and most considerate. It's impossible to judge human nature by the length of someone's driveway. That's the important thing this job's taught me: When it comes to people, the rule is—there's no rule.

I went into the cleaning business about ten years ago after losing my job with an accounting firm. [I'd been making fairly good money and was living well, and when I was exceptionally busy during tax time, I'd have a housekeeper come in and take care of my apartment. That's what gave me the idea of getting into the business.] It seemed like a good stop-gap thing to do while, at the same time, maintaining a degree of independence. So, I took on a few clients.

Well, today, I'm as busy as I want to be. Business is fantastic. I have seventeen people working for me. We service both industrial and residential. And the money's excellent. And I find the work much more challenging and cleaner than the accounting business any day.

Hey, if you think some of the places we service are a mess, you should check out a few tax returns.

AMY
(Pest Control)

Although Amy's job is highly anomalous for a woman, she is proud of her profession, and of the service she provides for her many clients.

AMY

I work for Termites, Incorporated. *(pointing proudly to an emblem on the collar of her coveralls)* See this? This is my five-year pin. It's a gold-plated termite. After ten years you get one with a ruby eyes. After fifteen they give you one with diamonds.

[One of the guys has a solid-gold termite with emeralds for eyes and diamonds all around the wings. He's been with the company for twenty-five years. He goes way back to the days when they still worked with DDT, before there was any great concern for the safety of the workers, the customers, or the environment. He's one of the pioneers, the old- timers, the daredevils. He has some great stories. I could listen to him talk all day long. He tells one story about the time he had this run-in with a bunch of gophers that's the wildest thing you've ever heard in your life. They nearly chewed him up before he got the best of them. You get a pack of gophers riled up, my friend, and you've got yourself a mess of trouble. They have teeth on 'em as sharp as razor blades.]

At Termites, Inc., we handle any pest problem you have: gopher control, flea elimination, cockroach eradication, ant control, ground squirrel elimination, cricket ridding, bee and wasp problems, mice and rat infestation, spider riddance, earwig elimination—the works! [And we'll take care of your grounds, too. We do tree spraying, take care of disease, control fungus, and control weeds and birds . . . you name it.]

Our methods are very scientific and state-of the-art. For instance: We stress biological and cultural techniques, using pesticides that'll do the least harm to the environment. [And we're especially careful when it comes to children and pets. Pets are highly susceptible to certain chemicals. I mean, you use something too lethal and you can have someone's poodle belly-up in no time. We had this one dip of a guy who used the wrong pesticide to knock out some carpet beetles and he wound up with a room full of dead cats.]

I just got back from mouse-proofing a house. The little creeps had fairly taken over the place. If you don't take care of mice they'll become as bold as door-to-door salesmen. You let 'em get out of hand and they'll wind up eating meals at your table.

The same with any vermin, any pest. The longer you let 'em go, the harder it is to eliminate them. They get into the cracks and crevasses and multiply. Especially fleas. You let fleas go, brother, and you'll have 'em dancing in your underwear.

[Pigeons can be a major problem, too. Oh yeah, you bet. They're one of the filthiest things on the face of the Earth. They may look cute from a distance, but when they move in, they come with family, friends, and baggage. And, boy, do they ever make a mess. They whitewash everything.]

[A good pest-control professional has to be ready, has to be available at all hours, seven days a week. Because your pests and your vermin have to be hit fast and hard and scientifically. We're at war with infestation around the clock because pests never rest. Do you think black widows and rats knock off for sleep at night? No way! They're gnawing and biting away on a twenty-four-hour basis.]

I'm proud of my record with Termites, Inc. When I leave a location, pests, insects, and vermin are at room temperature. They're feet are in the air. They're D-E-A-D! When I go in, I go in straight, and I go in hard, right into the face of the enemy. Yesterday I got dispatched to a house over on Snyder Street where termites were holding a national sales meeting under the foundation. Well, sir, I went right in there flat on my belly with pesticide blazing. And when I came out—the meeting was adjourned!

Of all the assignments, my least favorite is knocking out cockroaches. I don't know why, but cockroaches turn my stomach inside out. They're so damned slithery and creepy. And they feed on filth. Maybe that's the part that gets me; the locations that breed them. Like this restaurant I got a call to go to last week. When I pulled out the range, the whole wall behind it was alive; alive with cockroaches slithering over one another like black molasses running in all directions. I almost gagged. And not just because of the roaches. Because of the thought of people eating in a place like this. While I was at it, I should have eradicated the owner.

[But, this is part of it. It can't all be tree spraying and deep-root feeding, you know. In this profession you have to take the good, the bad, and the ugly. The only problem is—sometimes the ugly is yuck!]

EDIE
(Truck Driver—Long-Haul)

*Edie drives a semi, or a "large car" as the
drivers call them. She travels the States, picking
up loads and delivering. It's a grueling life—one
that borders on the monastic—requiring skill
and intelligence.*

EDIE

I drive out of South Bend for a large trucking
firm there. Last year I only worked eight
months, but I logged better than a hundred thousand miles. Since getting into the business I've
been on almost every interstate in the country
and most of the system's bypass and spur routes
and all kinds of divided and undivided state and
county roads. [Hell, they want something put on
a flyspeck at the end of a nowhere—I'll *be*
there. And on time.]

Trucking's a lonely business. You're out
there some damned place or the other most of

the time. Away from your home and your family. [The thing that gets to you the most is the fatigue factor and the sheer loneliness of the occupation. You know that the turnover in this business is almost forty percent?] A lot of gals just can't handle the isolation. It isn't the ideal job, but I had to get into something fast after my divorce.

I'm usually on the road by seven or eight every morning and sometimes I'll drive till midnight. On a good day I'll chalk up six or seven hundred miles. [These are the days I don't get hung up with loading and unloading and tarping and untarping or taking care of repairs or sitting around waiting for the dispatcher to find me a load. I haul mostly lumber, grinding balls, airplane parts, PVC pipe, big coils of steel, telephone cable, and the like—heavy stuff.]

Being on the road means you live on the run like some motorized gypsy. Most of the time I bed down in the back of the cab and my meals consist mostly of burgers and coffee, lots of coffee. A driver can forget all about gourmet meals. We have a saying: A seven-course dinner for a truck driver is a can of chili and a six-pack. [Sometimes, when I get over-tired or have a weekend layover someplace, I give myself a break and stay in a motel. Pretty boring, though. You just lie around the room and watch TV mostly. Or go to a movie if there's one in the area.]

I call my kids about three or four times a week. My phone calls home run about a hundred bucks a month. Sometimes, after ten hours of bad, wet, angry highway, the sound of your husband's voice is the only thing that keeps you from telling 'em to take the job and shove it.

I miss the kids. Three of 'em. A boy and two girls. We've got a little farm—ten acres—just outside South Bend. I don't get to spend as much time as I'd like to there and that's the thing that wears at me most. Here I am out here living like a hermit on wheels while everything I love or care about is two thousand miles away.

I'm driving extra time to salt away a few bucks and get off the road. Eventually, I want to set up a little business back home and live a regular life like other people. I've been out here on the road for a helluva long time. Longer than I ever thought.

What scares me the most is, if I'm not careful, I'm not gonna just be someone who's out here driving a truck, I'm gonna wind up being a truck driver.

DARLA
(Plumber)

The world of drains and traps and commodes is certainly not one of glamour. But Darla finds it interesting, challenging, and extremely lucrative.

DARLA

It seems like everybody makes plumber jokes, right? I get all kinds of handles attached to me: The Sultan of Sludge, The Drain Surgeon, Captain Crap—you name it. It's part of the image. People see us as people in smelly coveralls covered with goo from head to toe, people with IQs and hat sizes that match. You talk about your prejudice. [Last week my husband and I were at this party and when I was introduced as a plumber, people actually jumped back. I guess they thought I had a couple wads of wet hair on me, or something. Who knows? And, well . . . being a woman. . . .]

Of course, we do get into some pretty nasty situations. But all of our work isn't opening up a drain full of grease. We do a lot of contracting work, plumbing new-home projects, and the like. [There's a whole lot more to plumbing than running a snake down a drain. Master plumbers have to have a complete knowledge of many related factors.]

You make big money when you're called out on emergencies. But you earn it, believe me. Here you are, at home on Christmas, in the middle of checking out your new microwave, and you get this panic call from a woman who has a toilet stopped up. Her voice has this little catch in it and you can tell she's close to tears because she's got fourteen people in the house, including her mother-in-law, who don't have anywhere to get rid of Christmas dinner.

So, you drag out in the middle of a snow-storm and go to the house where there's a living room full of bloated-looking people. You have to open up the john, a job that, incidentally—in the interest of good taste—I won't describe in great detail. [Let's just say it's no bed of roses. After an hour, with your head in a quagmire, you get the thing open to the relief of all concerned. Then everybody thanks you and slaps you on the back and shakes your hand like you're this special person, like you're this savior, or something. For a couple of minutes there you're Albert Schweitzer. Then you hand them your bill, and alluva sudden you're the Grinch Who Stole Christmas.]

Plumbing's a rough job and you get into all kinds a situations with all kinds a people at all hours. [But this is what makes the job interesting—the variety of problems and the different types of people you meet. To be a successful plumber you have to be in touch with human nature, know how to read people and how to handle them. You have to be kind of like a pipe-wrench psychologist, you know.]

When you show up at someone's apartment at two o'clock on a cold morning and a bathtub's running over and the people downstairs are mad and screaming and kids are crying and the husband and wife are at each other's throats, you've got chaos on your hands, brother, and you've got to know what to do. And you've got to know how to handle the human element.

Let me tell you something: There's a lot more to plumbing than threading pipe.

LILLY
(Miner)

She was born and raised and still resides in a small mining town in western Pennsylvania where she, like most of the male population, grew into the miner's life. But Lilly has quit mining, is finished with the rigors and dangers below. Here, in a torrent of bitterness, frustration, and anguish, she speaks of mining and of her dad, who had fallen victim to one of the evils of "the hole."

LILLY

I was just a kid. But they were takin' women, and I was strong as a horse, so . . . what the hell? Everyone hereabouts went in t' the mines as soon as they were able; a lot of 'em still do. Why, what the hell else you gonna do, anyway? With a half-ass education an' bills you inherit from the time you're born. My daddy was a

51

miner an' his daddy before 'im. And my brothers. People tend t' be part o' where they are.

So, I was like the rest hereabouts. I got stuck in the hole, the stinkin' bottom o' the mother earth. Got shut up from the sunlight, penned up down there just like a human pig. I was seventeen when I went down. Just a girl. Tall an' straight with hair as thick an' black as tar. I went down smilin' an' came up without a dream. [There's no future in the hole. It's a place where ya get old before your time, where all ya have t' look forward to for the rest o' your life is a wall o' anthracite closin' in on your hopes like a big black vise.]

It's a life made by the devil t' trap ya. And it never gets better. Even though things are more modern t'day, the dangers are still there because there can't be guarantees when you're a thousand feet under ground. And the companies still don't give a damn—not really, they don't. They patch things up a bit here an' there an' make a big noise about it and call it improvement. Bullshit! Minin's still as dangerous as it ever was because profits still call the tune. So, the companies, they still cut corners. [They spend what they have to and no more and, at the same time, they talk about what they're doing for the miners an' how their so concerned for their safety.] They do a lot of bullshit PR so the general public won't know what's really going on underground.

Then there'll be a cave-in or a flood or an explosion an' there'll be miners trapped with no air an' timbers sawing their bodies in two. Then all the papers an' the TV jump on it an' the companies get scared shitless an' the big bosses run around crappin' in their pinstripes.

I'll never be able t' get out o' mind what the mines did t' m' daddy. Never. [The memory of it's just like a thick coat o' paint spread across the back o' my mind. Like his father, he didn't have a chance. He got born right in t' the midnight underground like most o' us. The mines were waitin' for 'im, just waitin' for 'im t' be born.] He worked in the hole till the black lung got 'im. He died before he was fifty. And his last couple o' years was a livin' hell. [For two years he could barely draw enough breath t' keep 'im going. For two years 'e had to suck hard for every ounce o' life.]

He never slept. He just set up in a straight chair gaspin' an' a-chokin' an' a-spittin'. He was full of it; full of the black death that was eatin' 'im up little by little. [And what could I do? Nothin'. Nothin' but sit by an' watch an' listen as 'is life was bein' squeezed.] An' he never said nothing. He never complained. But it was all in 'is eyes. The hell of it. The pain an' the sufferin' an' the regret. Sometimes I think the regret was the worst of it, the fact 'e never got out when 'e was young.

But it's over for me. I'm finished with the mines. I'm gittin' the hell out. If I don't, I'll either wind up like m' daddy, or busted up at the bottom of a shaft, or old before my time with a two-bit pension an' no dreams. I'm takin' m'self outta here while I still got a chance.

FLORENCE
(Painter)

Florence has learned that there is far more to her job than painting.

FLORENCE

I contract jobs of all kinds—from five hundred dollars to ten thousand. I go out and check out the situation and quote a price. Then we decide on the type of paint, the colors, and so on. New jobs—I mean new housing—are relatively easy. You work with the contractor and there aren't a heck of a lot of hassles. [I mean, here you've got ten condos and they all go a flat white with semi-gloss for trim, okay? A straight-ahead job. No problem.]

The killers are the smaller jobs where you get involved directly with the clients. For example: Here you've got this little old lady who lives in this house that's wall-to-wall with stuff she calls heirlooms that is actually junk. But to her, every piece is like the Crown Jewels. [You know, the kind of place where doilies are under everything, including the husband—this meek guy who sits around working a crossword while his wife takes you from room to room giving you a rundown on all of this fragile crap.]

She'll say, "See this platter? It belonged to my Aunt Edith. She was a Methodist who lived in Ft. Lauderdale. Her husband was a big man with the Elks who made big money in lumber before he had a car wreck that left him a vegetable. He had no control over his vital organs."

Then she takes you on this grand tour, commenting on everything and giving you background and details when you couldn't care less. ["This set of sandwich glass we've had since we went into housekeeping. Very valuable. Was a wedding gift from Jim's sister, Cora. She passed away last year up in Cleveland from choking on an Arby's beef sandwich. When I pass on, my niece gets it." Lucky girl. When the old lady expires, she inherits a truckload of glass that she gets the pleasure of dusting for the next fifty years.]

Of course, the reason she's telling me all this is so we'll be extra careful when we paint. Heaven forbid we nick a fifty-cent plaster of Paris doorstop. But, I listen and nod. I mean, what the hell? To her all this stuff's important. [And she's lonely. After all, who does she have to talk to? The lackluster guy sitting on a doily trying to figure out a four-letter word for intercourse? Forget it.]

Most people are very picky and finicky when it comes to painting. They deliberate and consider and haggle like crazy. You'd think they were getting a third opinion on major surgery. And they change their minds like crazy. Here you are right in the middle of a job when alluva sudden they'll decide that a periwinkle blue goes better than a cornflower yellow. Or that maybe, after seeing it on, they figure the lavender isn't going to pick up the background in the wallpaper.

I sometimes sit for hours with people while they deliberate and agonize over the paint charts. [They take them to the light and hold them up to drapes and carpets and furniture. And I've learned to never recommend. No way. Are you kidding? If you do, and they don't like the result—big trouble. So, I just sit back and listen and nod. What's it to me if they want to go for puce walls and a magenta ceiling? Hey, if they wanna turn their place into Santa's Village, it's their own damned business.]

Patience is one of the major requirements for being a painter. That and putting on this act like you're super-concerned. Of course, I figure all this in the price. It's part of my fee. After all, it's time, right? And time means dollars. And I don't come cheap. After all—good actors get paid big money.

JANE
(Auto Mechanic)

Jane, a prisoner to grease, has learned that a car is much more than a piece of machinery. It's "human."

JANE

They bring 'em in here and it's like they're human, ya know. Like they've got hearts and lungs and brains instead of engines and transmissions. They agonize over them like they're their children with whooping coughs and fevers. "She doesn't sound right, Jane," they'll say.

And I'll say, "How *does* she sound?"

And they'll say, "Ker-chunk-a-chunk-a-chank."

And I say, "Oh."

And they'll say, "Is that bad?"

And I say, "Well, not as bad as ker-plunk-a-plunk-a-clang." Then I pop the hood and look inside and the customer bends in over me so close I can tell what kind a dressing he had on his salad. Then I go, "Oh, ah."

And they go, "Ah, oh."

I go, "Hum."

And they go, "Um."

It's like this ritual, you know. But it's important because it makes 'em think their car's special and that you're super-concerned and it puts their minds at ease. [So, I treat the car like it's their pet poodle and look concerned and serious and close the hood carefully so as not to bruise it. You never drop a hood in front of the customer. Too brutal.]

The men are worse than the women because they think they know everything there is to know about automobiles. They read the reviews and the articles in the car magazines and this makes them experts—all Mario Andrettis. Of course, I never let on that they're wrong—which they are about ninety-five percent of the time. I just nod like I'm agreeing when they tell me the reason the car's not idling right is because the way gas is refined in America doesn't allow it to burn efficiently in the hemispherical combustion chamber. Hey, usually the reason the car's not idling properly is because the turkey hasn't changed the plugs in fifty thousand miles. [But I listen when they talk technical and go on about torque and sprung weight and fuel injection because I know it makes 'em feel better if they think they know more than I do. After they leave, we do what has to be done; which is usually basic stuff that's pretty much what we've been doing to cars since the Model T. Sophisticated technology usually isn't at the bottom of automotive problems.]

We repair mostly high-priced imports. But grease is still grease. [The grease from a Mercedes is just as impossible to wash off as the grease from a rusted-out Pinto. And after a few years it gets ground in, permanently imbedded, too. My hands will never be totally clean again. I've resigned myself to a life of dirty cuticles.]

I've scrubbed with every solvent known to man. Still, imbedded grease stands out in every line like these little black rivers. Look. *(displays her hands, palms up.)* Is this a fortune teller's dream, or what? I've tried everything. [You name it. Even Clorox. I thought I could bleach out the grime. No luck. All I did was wind up smelling like a laundry.]

I'm very self-conscious about my hands. But not nearly as much as I used to be. I used to hide them by keeping them in my pockets or behind my back. It was one hell of a crippling blow to my sex life, let me tell you, because men are turned off by greasy mitts.

Thank God I finally found one who wasn't. We were married last October. He's a transmission specialist for Aamco.

VERA
(Dishwasher)

Vera, on the rebound from drink, finds dishwashing excellent therapy.

VERA

I come in around four in the afternoon, before the dinner hour. We get the big push around six. I come in and help clean up the kitchen and get things in order. Everything in a kitchen has to run like on greased wheels, ya know. It has to have organization and be coordinated. [And everybody has a part. From the chef on down: The salad makers, the pastry chef, the steam table people, the people who work the grilles, the dishwashers—everybody. It's like this mechanized, assembly-line thing where everything has to come off smooth and without a hitch. When it hits the fan back here, all fucking hell breaks loose and you have to be ready to handle the peak business.]

I've got the lowest job in the kitchen—cleaning up the plates. [I have to scrub 'em and get 'em steam-cleaned and stacked and ready for the cooks. It's a tough, sweaty job but real important because if they're aren't any dishes, people don't eat, okay?]

Even though it's the lowest job, it's good because it's something and because now I'm working and making my way instead of sitting in a gutter someplace with a bag full of cheap wine and no future. That's the way it was for me for years—no tomorrow. Hell, time wasn't anything to me, period. Minutes and hours and days were all locked up in a drunken haze, and I got by by bummin' change and sleeping in doorways. All I was was a rag-bag, no-hope, whiskey-brained hunk of nothing. Until I got this job I was a living dead woman with no place to die.

The guy who owns the place, Sam Weller, he got me up off the street one night and got me a decent meal and offered me work. He said he'd take a chance on me if I was willing to take care of business and get my head out of my ass and get off the juice. [Sam's a tough guy, but at the same time he cares. And with him there's no bullshit. So, he put me here in the kitchen and I've been here over a year, and I haven't had a taste since last January.]

I almost went off the wagon a couple of times, but I hung tough. I had to. I mean, hell, a person can't go disappointing a guy like Sam, now, can she? It just wouldn't be right. After all, he believed in me and he taught me a lesson. He taught me that honest work can make your life mean something. Sam gave me hope.

Hell . . . the man gave me a life.

RUTH
(Cowgirl)

She dispels the idea that working the range is a glamour job.

RUTH

I'm up at daybreak twelve months a year. And I roll the hell out in all kinds a weather. Rain, sun, sleet, blizzards—you name it. [The snow can be up to yer buns an' you still gotta go out an' take care-a the heard.]

It's a hard life out here, mister. And fer chickenshit money an' no benefits. You gotta love this kind a life t' put up with it; gotta love the freedom of not havin' t' deal with people on a reg'lar basis. I'll take me a mean-ass steer over a weasel wearin' a necktie any day a the week. But the job's still a downright killer suited fer only a few crazy, hard-knockin' bitches like me.

People have this here idea about cowboys, ya know. They git it from yer books and yer TV and yer movies, an' the like. [They think it's all like yer John Wayne an' yer Gary Cooper an' yer Matt Dillon, an' the like. Hey, all this is twenty tons a horsemanure. Them's Hollywood cowboys!] Everone's got the idee all it is is a-savin' the ranch and blowin' holes in the rustlers an' screwin' the rancher's daughter. *(chuckles)*

[Do you realize that the cowboy was the first American hobo? Yep, you heard right—hobo—a drifter who worked. A misfit who couldn't live with other people, couldn't settle, couldn't git a holt on life, a loner who would rather drift an' poke longhorns an' smell bad an' sleep in his boots an' eat cold beans than put up with the rest a the civilized world. Was a person couldn't adjust, so he became an outsider.]

There ain't nothin' glamorous 'bout bein' a cowpoke. Hell no, never was. That there shit's all outta celluloid, all parta thc glamour image put out by the Hollywood motion picture business. People have the notion that the cowboy won the West.

Hell, the cowboy didn't win the fucking West, the railroads won the fucking West. They think he run out the fucking outlaws. Hell, he didn't run out the fucking outlaws, the fucking outlaws became fucking business men. They think he took care-a the Indians. Hell, he didn't take care-a the Indians, the fucking Army took care-a the Indians. The cowboy didn't do nothing but work 'is butt off an' eat dust an' git saddle sores.

An' ever'one's Western crazy these days, too. Everbody's runnin' around wearin' Levis an' workshirts an' Western hats an' boots. The cowboy's big with the fashion set because they've been convinced that this here is the life. I'd laugh if I didn't think I'd puke. *(chuckles at the thought of it)*

I'd like to see these here Polo and Guess Jeans cowboys and cowgirls out here in their thousand-dollar alligators an' designer pants. Hell, 'bout the first zero, bone-cold mornin' they had to roll out into a pile a steer shit, they'd be back to their BMWs in no time.

CARLA
(Mail Carrier)

Carla, on the same swing (route) for years, has keen perception relative to her occupation.

CARLA

I've been carrying mail on this route for nearly ten years. And neither storm and rain and snow and hail—nothing—has deterred me once from making my appointed rounds. [No, sir. I get the mail to the house, in the slot, regardless. It's my job.]

People are downright nuts, fanatics when it comes to their mail. Like it's the most important thing in their lives, you know. I guess this says a whole lot about the human condition, huh? And most of the time all they ever receive is crap: bulletins, catalogs, flyers—promotional junk. Hell, half of the stuff in my bag is nothing but pure unadulterated doggie ca-ca. [And when you get this stuff together, it weights a ton, too.

(massages her lower back gingerly) I've got these direct-mail retail sharks to thank for a bad fifth lumbar.]

After all of these years, I know most of the people on my swing intimately. It's like I've become part of their family. In some cases, in fact, I *am* family.

Like this one little old woman over on Maple Street, Mrs. Cartmell. Sometimes I think I'm the only friend she has on the planet. Her kids never come to see her—nobody. Only me, Clara Withers, U. S. Postal Service carrier number ten twenty-five. Other than me, the poor woman's a forgotten soul, a dried-up piece of yesterday sitting in her window staring out at the past. She looks forward to me coming every day and always has coffee for me, or iced tea, or something like that. The other day she baked cinnamon rolls. I always spend a few minutes with her and listen to her problems. It's the least I can do.

In December the job really gets crazy, because people who don't communicate all year long send out Christmas cards. Mr. Hallmark is making a fortune. ["When you care enough to send the very best." I've kind of changed that around: "When you don't care enough to spend money for a long-distance call." Sometimes, during the holidays, the load's so heavy I have to make two swings a day.]

At Christmas time I usually get a gift here and there. Cookies, candy, ties, cash. Cash is always welcome. Green goes well with everything. Mrs. Jamison, over on Whipple Avenue, she gave me fifty bucks last year. A hot-looking guy down on Elm Street wanted to give me more than that—if you know what I mean. But I don't make those kinds of deliveries.

I guess some men just can't resist a woman in uniform.

SALLY
(Farmer)

She reflects upon farm life, her father, tradition.

SALLY

I come down here every evening after the work is done. To be alone and reflect on the land. It's my way of paying homage, my way of paying respects.

It was my father who taught me to respect the land. In fact, he's the one who got me into the habit of coming down here like this. He used to every evening, regardless of the weather, no matter what.

I can see him now: Standing here with his cap in his hands, his hair blowing around his face. I remember how he squinted out over the fields, how he scanned the horizon and the woods and the distant silos of neighboring farms. He would be all concentration and focus. He would take it all in as if he were inhaling it through his eyes. I didn't understand it then, but, as I grew up working the farm, I came to know the reason for his daily meditations.

[I think to be a good farmer you have to have a love affair with the land. You have to have this feeling for it that connects you to it in a spiritual way. You have to relate to it as the giver and the life force.]

My father was only an eighth-grade-educated man. He didn't have the advantage—an advantage I received because of him—of an education. But maybe . . . maybe in some ways, he was the one who had an advantage because he wasn't schooled. Sometimes, if you're not careful how you handle it, too much education can cloud real feelings, can dirty up the pure waters. *(pause)* Yep, my dad definitely had an edge in the feeling department, all right.

Even though farming's a hard life, it's a good life. Good because there's this directness to it, this clean edge, this simplicity. [When you complete a day out here, you complete it with an act of finality. It's like splitting a piece of dry hickory. You know it's over. You know it's complete.]

When I stand here, when I look out over the fields and smell the earth, and feel the wind and the sun and the rain and all of the little-big things that make nature special, I know I'm blessed, I know that farming is a special thing. And from here I can see the little cemetery up near the maple grove where Dad is buried— where he sleeps under the land he loved so much.

I'm proud to be a farmer, and prouder to be his daughter.